where
we
live

Prestel

In the beginning there was the cave...

Thousands of years ago people probably lived in simple shelters made of branches and straw. No one knows for sure because after such a long time not much is left of these dwellings for scientists to analyze.

Sometimes our ancestors found shelter in natural caves, where we can find remnants of bones and fire pits even today.

Also, we can admire the beautiful images that our ancestors painted onto the cave walls.

Scientists imagine that the simple huts where people lived 400,000 years ago looked something like this. This picture shows a reconstruction.

Surprisingly enough, hundred of thousands of people still live in caves, which they use as underground houses. But now people build and expand their caves to have more space.

In this small picture you can see modern "cave people" in Matmata, Tunisia. They live in caves that they have dug by themselves into the earth and enlarged into apartments.

3

Houses without doors— how would you get in (or out)?

A long, long time ago people started planting fields instead of only gathering food in the wild. They no longer only hunted wild animals, but kept their own herds as well. They were ready to live in one place and stay there.

If you do not have to travel around all the time to look for plants and animals in the wild, you no longer need houses—like tents—that are light enough to carry with you.

And so one of the first cities came to be built in about 6,000 BC. It is called Çatal Hüyük. The ruins of the city have been discovered in modern-day Turkey. The illustration to the left shows a model of Çatal Hüyük. The houses were made of clay bricks and were rectangular, all for the very first time.

They were also built together. In other words, one house was attached to the next. That means they didn't have to build as many walls. It also means that there were no city streets: people ran around on the rooftops! If they wanted to get into a house, they just climbed through a hole (like a submarine hatch) and stepped down a ladder.

One special advantage to this was that anyone who wanted to get into the city from outside had to bring a ladder to get up onto a roof first. And this made the inhabitants of Çatal Hüyük feel very safe.

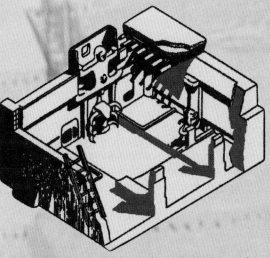

Inside there were adobe (clay) platforms instead of chairs, tables, and beds. The platforms were covered in furs and the spaces underneath them were used as places of burial for the dead.

The inhabitants of Çatal Hüyük were probably the first people ever to draw a "city map." In the background, you can see the fire-spewing volcano called Hasan Dag.

Today, there are modern city neighborhoods which look very much like that ancient city; they look like "boxes" piled on top of each other.

In the picture you see a modern example: it is called "Habitat Flats" and was designed by Moshe Safdie (in Montreal in 1966/67).

5

What is the Eskimo word for "house"?

Most people think that Eskimos (or Inuit, as they prefer to be called) live in igloos. That's not really quite true. For most of the year they live in huts made of earth and turf or driftwood. In another way, though, people are right, because in their native language all houses are called "igloo"!

When the Eskimos go off on their hunting trips across the huge expanse of ice, they are often away from home for weeks at a time. To keep warm and snug, and to protect themselves from the giant polar bears, they build houses out of snow—the houses that we call igloos. Since there is nothing else around, they carve blocks out of packed snow and put them on top of each other to make a dome. This is the best shape to build. Just imagine having to make a house with straight walls out of snow: in the end, you would have to cut one very large block of snow to make a roof—and you can be sure it would cave in.

The easiest way to build is to make the walls and ceiling run into each other, creating the rounded shape we all know.

Although snow is freezing cold, it is possible to make the inside warm and cozy. When several Eskimos are together in their igloo and a petroleum lamp is burning, their snow-house soon warms up nicely. The snow walls keep all the warmth in (and the cold out).

The name "Eskimo" actually means "eater of raw meat." The Eskimos call themselves Inuit, which means "man" or "person" in English.

Why are igloos egg-shaped?

Take a raw egg and roll it across a lawn. It won't break. That's because the shape of an egg is almost, but not quite, like a ball. And the ball shape is the sturdiest shape there is. An igloo looks like half an egg, and it's just as solid. Even a polar bear can stand on top of it!

What is probably the world's largest igloo is in Norway. It is a hotel made of snow and ice that is rebuilt every winter. Even the beds, tables, and chairs are carved out of ice.

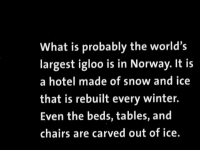

Houses for buffalo hunters...

Not all Native Americans lived in tents (or tepees, as they call them). Only those Indian nations which hunted and followed the wild buffalo herds built themselves tepees with long wooden poles and leather skins, which were left over after the hunters had eaten all the buffalo meat or dried it for food in the winter month Tepees have a small hole at the very top where the smoke can flow out—like igloos.

The tents are so light that they can be transported on horseback without any problem.

People all around the world have always had tents, and still have them today—especially people who move around a lot, like the Native Americans used to when they were following the buffalo. These people are called nomads. Many nomads are in fact shepherds who are moving along with a herd

from one fresh grazing ground to another. Tents come in many different shapes, colors, and sizes, depending on local traditions and uses of the tent.

If you've ever traveled with a tent before, you know just how practical it is to have your "home" with you wherever you go.

epees are very easy to take down and set up again in a new spot. This was very important for the Native Americans every time the buffalo moved on. To hunt buffalo you've got to go where they go!

In this picture, you can see all the parts you need to build a tepee. Three thick wooden poles make up the basic frame. The open spaces in between are filled with thinner poles. Finally, the whole frame is covered by a blanket made of buffalo skin.

Today we no longer need buffalo skins to make tents. Instead, the "skins" we use are called membranes, a man-made material. We also use hollow metal poles instead of wooden ones. But the basic idea is still the same: whenever we have to build a house very quickly, we build a tent with a thin sheet that is stretched across poles. And because we no longer hunt buffalo, but go camping instead, we use nylon fabrics. They are lighter than buffalo leather and very easy to buy in modern cities.

9

Home address: jungle, tenth floor

Solid, thick walls aren't the only way of protecting yourself against enemies. Other people have a completely different strategy—because in the jungle and in swamps they are surrounded not only by wild animals but also by hostile neighbors and diseases.

The Korowai people live in the dense jungles of Papua New Guinea, where they build their houses high up in the trees. Usually, they are afraid of their neighbors.

It's easy to tell whether people are fighting in their land: you just have to look at how high the houses are built in the trees. When there's peace the houses are built much lower.

But when the neighbors are on the warpath, the houses virtually disappear into the treetops.

he tree houses are built with wooden poles and palm eaves; the floors are made of bark. The Korowai have either ropes nor nails: their complicated structures are ed together with vines, and because they are quite large, hey are also propped up by long wooden posts.

The Korowai raise pigs and also keep other domestic animals up in their homes in the sky. If one of their dogs has to "go for a walk," a Korowai just takes him outside for a moment.

Korowai tree house (top).

In Holland there are modern "tree houses" right in the middle of the city. Actually, they are more like house trees or artificial trees, because they are not built in trees, but look like trees themselves (below).

Living on stilts!

You can live on stilts without teetering above the ground at the same dizzying heights as the Korowai people. Most buildings on stilts are not very high at all. What really matters is that the buildings are raised. Putting your house on stilts is a good idea in regions where the ground is wet, swampy, and muddy, or where the ground is simply not there—like in the middle of a lake. You have to build your house on stilts if you don't want to get your feet wet!

Some 1,550 years ago, a group of people fled to a marshy area in a lagoon to escape their enemies. They started to build a whole city on stilts, something that went on for many hundreds of years. Today that city is known as Venice.

But why do some people choose to live in a wet and swampy area when they want to keep dry in the first place? Well, one reason is that many people around the world make a living from fishing, and it makes things easier to live where the fish are found.

Others choose to live in places where you really need to protect yourself to be able to live there at all. Often this is because of a fear of other people or animals.

Houses on stilts have been built all over the world since prehistoric times. Many years ago, a little boy who was living in Switzerland heard about the discovery of some ancient structures on stilts. This child later became a famous architect called Le Corbusier and added stilts to some of his modern buildings. He found these structures to be light and airy, and also liked the idea of being able to drive under a house and park the car there!

Even in houses on stilts, nobody can be safe at all times. According to tales from a long time ago, children living on the water in ancient Greece were tied by one ankle to a pole to stop them from falling into the sea below while they played!

One of Le Corbusier's famous houses is the Villa Savoye near Paris. Only the entrance and the garage are on the ground floor—the rest of the house is supported on white poles.

Living next door to animals

Farmhouses have always been very important to any community because the farmers make sure that people have milk, eggs, grains, and meat to live on. For centuries farmhouses have been built so well and in such a practica manner that we can still learn from them today when we build new houses. Farmhouses were often built into slight depressions in the ground so that the wind would blow over the top. And trees and bushes were planted all around the house for further protection.

People and animals lived more or less under the same roo The "weather side" of the house, that is, the side against which the wind blows most often, was used for the stable. Cows, sheep, and pigs don't mind the cold because they have a thick fur or tummy fat. The animals even warm up the stable with their body

A farm in southern England.

The hay was stacked above the living areas to keep them nice and warm, like slipping underneath a thick blanket. The stove stood in the center of the farmhouse. The kitchen stove and the tiled stove in the living room were connected to it.

eat. This means that the stable on the weather side shelters the farmer's living area against the cold.

Not only did the farmer, his wife, and a few cows live in the ancient farmhouses: there were the farm maids, who fed the animals and washed the clothes; the farmhands, who mucked out the stable and brought in the hay, and many others …

An American farm with large grain silos.

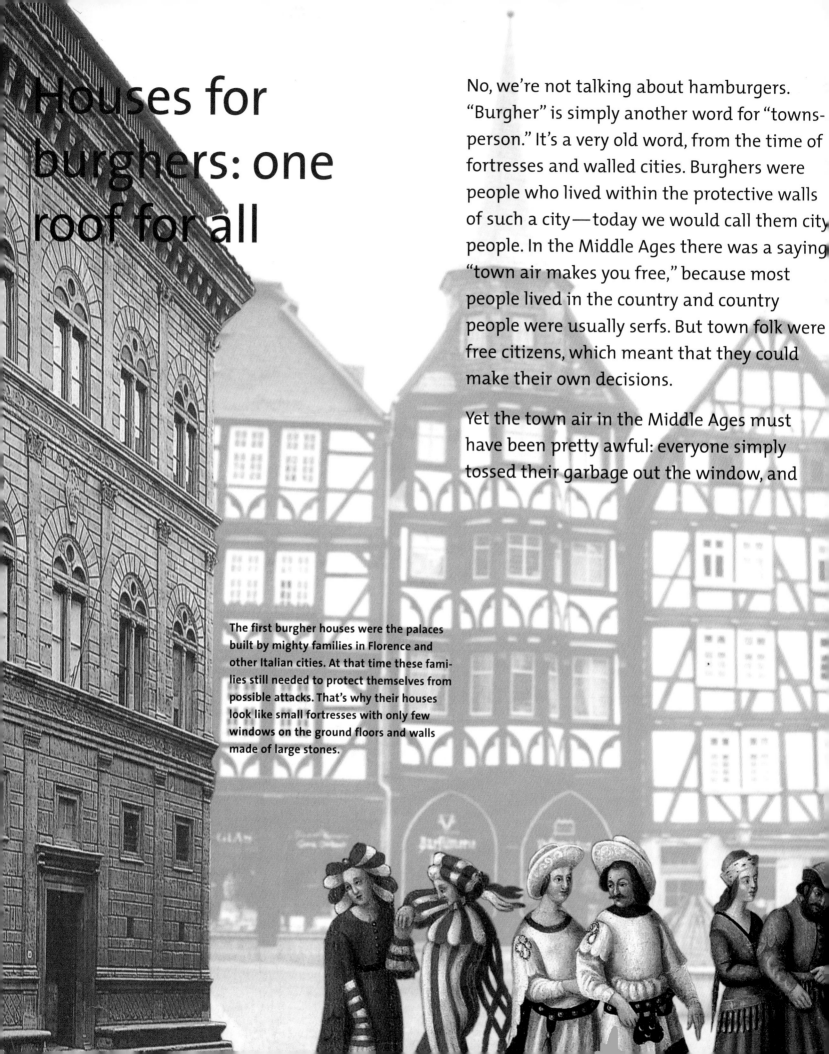

Houses for burghers: one roof for all

No, we're not talking about hamburgers. "Burgher" is simply another word for "towns-person." It's a very old word, from the time of fortresses and walled cities. Burghers were people who lived within the protective walls of such a city—today we would call them city people. In the Middle Ages there was a saying "town air makes you free," because most people lived in the country and country people were usually serfs. But town folk were free citizens, which meant that they could make their own decisions.

Yet the town air in the Middle Ages must have been pretty awful: everyone simply tossed their garbage out the window, and

The first burgher houses were the palaces built by mighty families in Florence and other Italian cities. At that time these families still needed to protect themselves from possible attacks. That's why their houses look like small fortresses with only few windows on the ground floors and walls made of large stones.

The only garbage collectors were the pigs that were herded through the narrow lanes. The houses themselves were narrow, too: the owner's shop or workshop was usually on the ground floor, with the bedrooms and living rooms above. But you mustn't imagine that these were separate living rooms, dining rooms, and bedrooms like we have today.

Often one room was used for everything: sleeping, eating, playing, and celebrating. A table was set up every day for mealtimes, and the beds were pulled out every night for sleeping. Many people shared the house—not just the family, but all the servants and employees, too. Often there were ten or twenty people living in one house, sometimes even fifty.

17

Why do castles have wings?

(And if so, why can't they fly?)

In the Middle Ages kings and counts were the leaders of the land. They built mighty fortresses into which all the people in the area could flee when there was danger. Many years later the fortresses no longer provided protection because cannons could reduce even the thickest walls to rubble and ashes.

And so the fortresses, which before had not been very comfortable to live in, were decorated, made more and more beautiful, and turned into castles. At first, most castles looked almost like normal houses, but over time other parts were added to them. Often these were long sections added on both sides of the house, called the "wings" of the castle, enclosing a beautiful courtyard. Castles, too, were houses where everyone lived under one roof: the servants and chambermaids, the grooms and soldiers, all shared the rooms in the wings.

The castle was a symbol visible from a great distance: Here lives the King! Three hundred years ago, there lived a king who was very good at building castles: Louis the Fourteenth, King of France. He built a beautiful castle called "Versailles" (you pronounce it "Vair-sigh"). There was no larger castle for miles and miles around. Louis organized many operas and festivals at Versailles and this kept the other princes so busy that they didn't have time to interfere with his politics. And because no one other than Louis had time to run the country, he became more and more powerful.

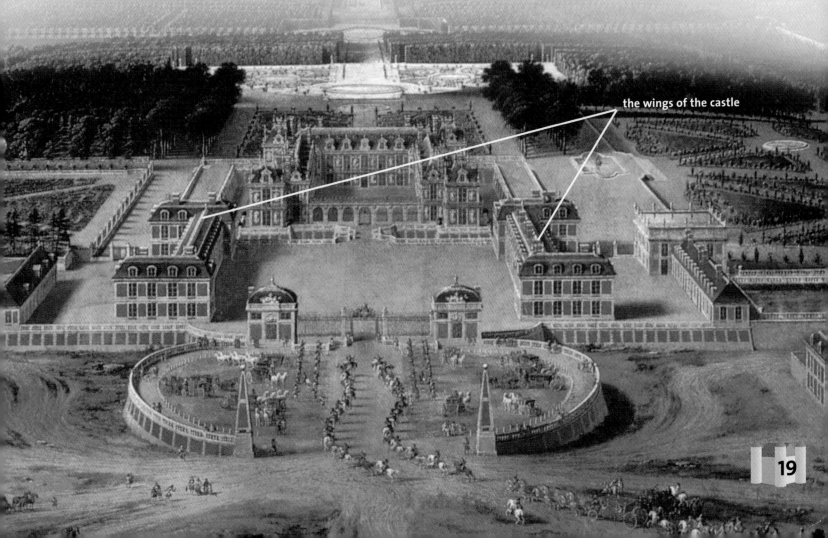

the wings of the castle

Mobile homes: following the snail's example

When Grandma and Grandpa were young, camping was also all the rage. This picture shows an aerodynamic caravan from the 1930s. The model was called "Aero Sport."

Since a very long time ago, the peoples called the Sinti and the Roma have moved around with their houses, which were once pulled along by horses. But they weren't the only people constantly moving from place to place. There were also traveling trades-men, tricksters, and gamblers, who came together to form traveling circus acts.

When cars were invented, it became much easier to take your house along with you. Now, anyone can travel across the countryside with a "house on their back," just like snails have always done.

Even standard homes can be strapped onto "roller skates" and moved around—provided they are not built of stone, because then they would be too heavy.

Roma camp from about 100 years ago.

Poster showing Circus Sarrasani on the move.

A mobile home in the
United States in the 1970s.

And in our basement, there are fish...

To live on a boat and to travel from port to port...

Most people who live on boats or house-boats don't really travel that much. So why do they need a boat?

The South Seas is a part of the world where small islands are surrounded by a lot of water. The people who live there are sea nomads, traveling *not* with horse and cart or with camels (which are sometimes called the ships of the desert) but with a boat.

In crowded Hong Kong there probably wouldn't be enough space if everyone wanted to live on land.

In many areas of Asia, rivers are the most important "roads." Many people live and work on the river, and so they need a boat.

In Europe and in North America people simply *like* to live near the water. What could be more wonderful than a house-boat—in Seattle, for example?

Dreams and Reality

Today we live in single-family houses or apartment buildings, and if you really want to peer down onto the world below, you live in a skyscraper. Most people would probably prefer to live in a house of their own, where it is nice and quiet and not so crowded. But a single-family house can cost a lot of money, and not everyone can afford to live in one. There is a good side to this—single-family houses take up a lot of space, and if everybody had one, more and more would be built, covering all of the fields, meadows, and forests. But wasn't it the desire for space that made people want single-family houses in the first place?

It is actually a good thing that many people like to live amidst the hustle and bustle of cities. Apartment buildings provide an efficient way of living together, because so many are able to live in a small area. And, of course, an apartment building environment can have many of the nice things we think of when we imagine living in nature, such as trees, birds, nice lawns, and flowers. In densely settled cities, where lots of people live in a small area, apartment

One person builds the house of her dreams in the green…

Buildings are sometimes so high that they scrape the sky!

Although many people can live in one skyscraper, they are very expensive to build, much more costly than a four- or five-floor apartment building.

So what are some other reasons to build skyscrapers?

Perhaps it is simply the fascination with being up so high, the exciting feeling of being able to look down on the world below, where the people and cars are so small that they look as though they are not real, but just toys instead…

…others live close to one another where there is always something going on…

…and when it gets really crowded, we build higher and higher, until we almost touch the sky!

25

Or something completely different…?

Houses come in all shapes and sizes. And that's a good thing because people do too. Some houses are only in your mind. Fantasies like that are called utopia, which more or less translates as "an ideal place"—or a house that exists only in your imagination. The word "utopia" comes from a 500-year-old story, which tells of a dream land, an ideal state or country. Throughout history, people have tried to think of how everything could be different. Some of those ideas have become reality; if not we would still be living in straw huts.

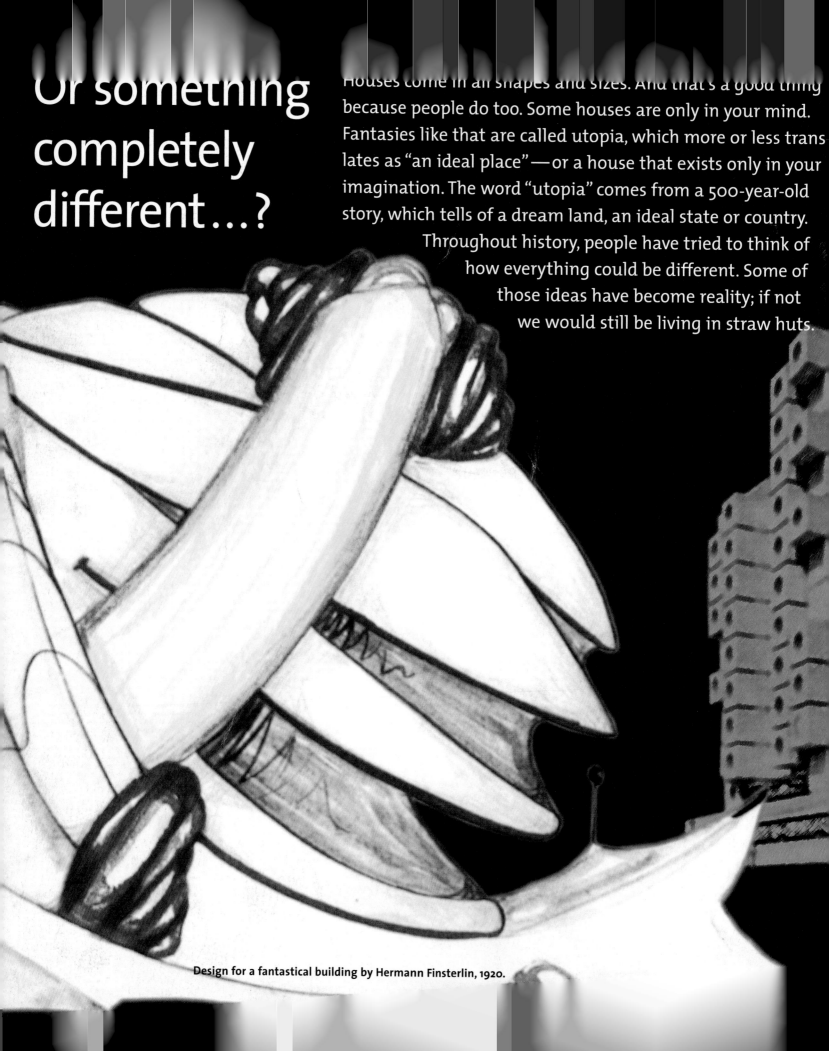

Design for a fantastical building by Hermann Finsterlin, 1920.

Some people with utopian ideas have imagined cars driving over rooftops, and others imagined entire cities walking about on the move. In some fantasies people live in man-size cans that they can stick inside high-rises all over the world, while other utopians are convinced that cities need more plants to improve the air and make them less gray. How would you like to live? There are endless possibilities. And they are all good as long as you feel comfortable.

Remember: even the small boy who later became the famous architect Le Corbusier had wild ideas in his head about how people could live in totally different houses—and he didn't let anyone tell him otherwise!

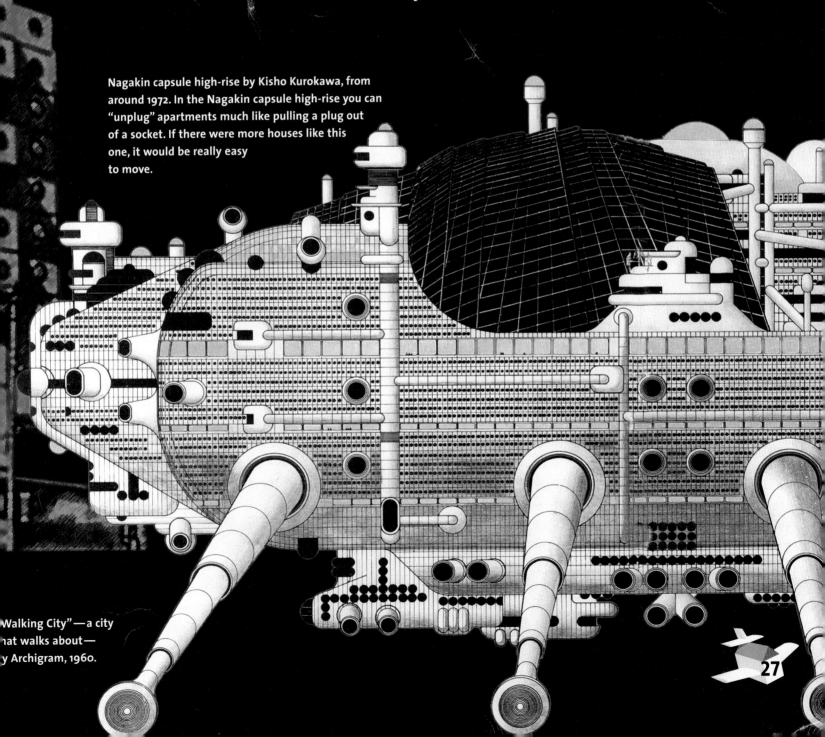

Nagakin capsule high-rise by Kisho Kurokawa, from around 1972. In the Nagakin capsule high-rise you can "unplug" apartments much like pulling a plug out of a socket. If there were more houses like this one, it would be really easy to move.

Walking City"—a city that walks about— y Archigram, 1960.